Date Due

A SUMMARY OF THE
LITERATURES OF
MODERN EUROPE

A SUMMARY OF THE LITERATURES OF MODERN EUROPE

(ENGLAND, FRANCE, GERMANY, ITALY, SPAIN)

FROM THE ORIGINS TO 1400

COMPILED AND ARRANGED BY

MARIAN EDWARDES

J. M. DENT & CO.
ALDINE HOUSE, BEDFORD STREET, LONDON
1907

INTRODUCTORY NOTE

To the wayfarer through an unfamiliar country there is
no more welcome sight than a sign-post. The present work
aims at nothing beyond fulfilling the office of a sign-post to
the inexperienced traveller along the roads and by-ways of
literature. It is intended to lighten as far as possible the
preliminary labour that has to be gone through before the
real business of literature may be said to begin, and to
that end solely it has been prepared. It seemed possible to
the compiler to save much waste of time and trouble to
students by providing a serviceable outline on which to base
a further study of the literatures dealt with in this volume;
but, it need hardly be said, within the limits of the forth-
coming pages an outline alone was possible. To glance
through the table of contents of a number or two of
"Romania," or any kindred journal, is sufficient to become
aware how great is the mass of literature which has gathered
round the vernacular writings of the west of Europe. It will
be further understood that only an indication could be given
of the various theories connected with the chief points of
controversy. Finally, the bibliography is select rather than
exhaustive, but this can be pretty fully completed with the
help of the books given under the heading of "General

Authorities " and of those mentioned under the separate works. The working value and service of a book of this kind can only be tested by those who use it.   If this compilation should in any measure help those who need map, or landmark, in starting their literary studies, it will have well carried out its intent.   And even if it does not wholly fulfil the design with which it was arranged, it may serve to clear the way for some future work which will more fully accomplish this purpose.

M. E.

MSS. IN ENGLISH LIBRARIES, Etc.

BRITISH MUSEUM—
    Additional.
    Arundel.
    Cotton (Jul., Cal., Vesp.,
       etc.).
    Egerton.
    Harley.
    Lansdowne.
    Sloane.
    Stowe.
    Royal (Reg.).

BODLEIAN—
    Ashmole.
    Bodley.
    Digby.
    Douce.
    Fairfax.
    Junius.
    Laud.
    Selden.
    Tanner.
    Vernon.

Phillipps MSS.—At Thirlestaine House, Cheltenham.

Ashburnham MSS.—Now dispersed.

Textus Roffensis.—MSS. belonging to the Collection of Charters, Anglo-Saxon and Anglo-Norman Laws, Records of Archbishops and Bishops of England, collected by Ernulf of Beauvais, Bishop of Rochester (1040–1124) preserved at Rochester.

N.B.—Reference to injury or destruction by fire.—In 1731 the Cotton Collection was seriously damaged and in part destroyed by a fire at Ashburnham House where the MSS. were at that time lodged.

ABBREVIATIONS.

C.C.C.C.—Cambridge, Corpus Christi College.

E.E.T.S.—Early English Text Society, founded by Dr. F. J. Furnivall, 1864.

Saxon and Middle English Texts are published in the "Albion" Series, ed. by Professors Bright and Kittredge (Ginn) and in the "Belles Lettres" Series, ed. by Prof. G. M. Brown (Heath).

Dict. Nat. Bio.—Dictionary of National Biography, ed. by Leslie Stephen & Sidney Lee, 1885, etc.

———————————

Works marked * are published in the Rolls Series: "Rerum Britannicarum Medii Aevi Scriptores," or, "Chronicles and Memorials of Great Britain and Ireland."

TABLE OF CONTENTS

ENGLAND.

ix

FRANCE.

VIIITH TO XTH CENTURY.

XITH CENTURY.

XIITH CENTURY.

ENGLAND

PERIODS OF LITERATURE

DIVISION ACCORDING TO KÖRTING
(*Grundrisz der Geschichte der Englischen Literatur*).

ANGLO-SAXON, OR OLD ENGLISH,
FROM THE ORIGINS TO CIR. MIDDLE 11TH CENTURY (1066).

TRANSITIONAL, OR EARLY MIDDLE ENGLISH,
FROM THE CONQUEST TO CIR. MIDDLE 13TH CENTURY.

MIDDLE ENGLISH,
CIR. MIDDLE 13TH CENTURY TO CIR. MIDDLE 14TH.

LATE MIDDLE ENGLISH,
CIR. MIDDLE 14TH TO CIR. BEGINNING OF 16TH CENTURY.

ANOTHER DIVISION
(See Hadley & Kittredge, *Introd. to Webster's Internat. Dict.*).

ANGLO-SAXON,
PERIOD OF FULL INFLEXION, 450–1150.

SEMI-SAXON,
INFLEXION IN GREAT MEASURE RETAINED, 1150–1250.

OLD ENGLISH,
INFLEXION TO A GREAT EXTENT DISCARDED, 1250–1350.

MIDDLE ENGLISH,
1350–1550.

LIST OF GENERAL AUTHORITIES.

G. Körting, "Grundrisz der Geschichte der Eng. Litteratur," 4th ed., 1905; Paul, "Grundrisz der Germanischen Philologie" (Eng. section, Ten Brink and Brandl), Bd. ii. Abth. i.; H. Morley, "First Sketch of Eng. Literature," 1886, 1901; "English Writers," 1887, 1888; Ten Brink, "Geschichte der Eng. Litteratur," 1873, 1893; 2nd. ed., vol. i., Brandl, 1899; Eng. trans., Kennedy (vol. i.); Clarke Robinson (vol. ii.), 1883, 1893; Kögel, "Geschichte der deutschen Litteratur bis zum Ausgange des Mittelalters," 1894, etc.; Wülcker, "Gesch. der Eng. Litt. von den Anfängen," 1896; R. Garnett, "English Literature," vol. i., 1903; Courthope, "History of Eng. Poetry," vol. i., 1895; Saintsbury, "A Short History of Eng. Lit.," 1903; Wright, "Biographia Britannica Literaria," 1842-9.

A.-S. PERIOD.—Earle, "A.-S. Literature," 1884; Wülcker, "Grundrisz zur Gesch. A.-S. Litt.," 1885; A. S. Brooke, "History of Eng. Lit. to King Alfred," 1892; "Eng. Lit. to the Norman Conquest," 1898; Ebert, "Allgemeine Gesch. der Litt. des Mittelalters, etc.," vol. iii., 1887; Sharon Turner, "Hist. of the Anglo-Saxons, etc.," 1799-1805.

TEXTS.—Grein, "Bibliothek der A.-S. Poesie," 4 vols., 1857-64; revised, Wülcker, 1883, etc.; "Bibl. A.-S. Prosa" (cont. by Wülcker), 6 vols., 1872-1905; Wülcker, "Kleinere A.-S. Dichtungen," 1882; Sweet, "Oldest English Texts," E.E.T.S., 1885; Morris, "Specimens of Early English," 1866; ed. Skeat, 1882, 1885; Thorpe, "Analecta Ang.-Saxonica," 1834, 1846; Conybeare, "Illustrations of A.-S. Poetry," 1826; Mätzner, "Alt-Englische Sprachproben," 1867; Selections in Readers by Sweet, Earle, Cook, Baskervill, Bright, Zupitza, and Maclean (based on Zupitza).

ROMANCES.—Ritson, "Ancient Metrical Romances," 1802; Weber, "Metrical Rom. of the 13th, 14th, and 15th Centuries," 1810; Hartshorne, "Ancient Metrical Tales," 1829; Halliwell, "Thornton Romances," 1844; Ellis, "Specimens of Early English Metrical Romances," revised Halliwell, 1847.

The above works will be referred to as *op. cit.* The collections of Grein-Wülcker being complete will not be referred to under separate A.-S. works.

BIBLIOGRAPHY.—Complete in Paul, and Körting; *see* also Chevalier, "Bio-bibliographie," 1905, etc. (for English and foreign authors).

ENGLAND

ANGLO-SAXON PERIOD

Settlement of Teutonic Tribes in Britain.

The hordes of warlike Teutons who invaded Britain in the 5th century were composed of Angles, Saxons, Jutes, and Frisians. These four tribes established themselves in different parts of the island, and the close of the following century found the Saxons settled in the South (Essex, Sussex, Middlesex, Wessex), the Jutes and Frisians in Kent and the Isle of Wight, and the Angles in Norfolk and Suffolk, and spreading northward as far as the South East of Scotland; the West still remained in possession of the Celt.

Early Centres of Culture.

A.D. 597. S. Augustine landed in England. The two great centres of culture, during the period which followed upon the introduction of Christianity into the country, were the schools of Kent and the schools of York; these flourished until the land became devastated by the inroads of the Danes.

Dialects.

The chief dialects of the Teutonic settlers were: the Northumbrian in the North; the Mercian in the centre; the Kentish, which was the first to be associated with a literary form; and the West Saxon, the latter being confirmed in its pre-eminence by the writings of Aelfred and Aelfric.

N.B.—Anglo-Saxon remains are extant only in Southern (Wessex) transcriptions, but it is more than probable that they originated in the North (Horstmann).

1 The two most important extant collections of A.-S. prose and poetry are—

1 *The Exeter Book* (Codex Exoniensis). This book was presented to his Cathedral by Leofric, the first Bishop of Exeter, about the middle of the 11th century. It is preserved in the Cathedral Library at Exeter; the first leaves are missing, and the last leaves are injured; the handwriting of the MS. belongs probably to the first half of the 11th century. *Ed.*, with trans., B. Thorpe, 1842; I. Gollancz, Poems i. to viii., E.E.T.S., 1895.

2 *The Vercelli Book* (Codex Vercellensis). Discovered by Dr. Blume, at Vercelli, N. Italy, in 1822. It is distinguished from the Exeter Book by containing prose (Homilies, Life of S. Guthlac) as well as verse. The MS. dates probably from the early 11th century, and is in two, or, perhaps, three handwritings. *Ed.*, Text of poems (with trans.), J. M. Kemble, 1843–56; R. Wülcker 1894 (photo. facsimile of verse).[1] *See* A. S. Cook, "Cardinal Guala and the Vercelli Book," and Introduction to his ed. of "The Dream of the Rood," 1904.

CHARACTERISTICS OF A.-S. POETRY.

The most striking characteristics of A.-S. Poetry are: inversion of phrase; redundance of metaphor; "parallelism," or repetition in synonymous terms of the same fact or idea. Both rhyme and alliteration are found in A.-S. Poetry, but rhyme is less generally introduced. The structure of the verse is trochaic; the line is divided into two halves by the Cæsura, each half line having two stressed syllables, the unstressed syllables varying in number; the half lines are associated by alliteration, one stressed syllable at least in each half line beginning with a similar consonant, or vowel. Usually the alliteration falls on the two stressed syllables in the first half line and the first stressed syllable in the second.

[1] The editions of the Exeter and Vercelli Codices will not be referred to under the separate poems contained in them.

2   Earliest extant A.-S. poems, of uncertain date, and still preserving pagan elements.[1]

Widsith (far-traveller), sometimes called "The Traveller's Song," or "The Scop, or Scald's Tale."

The travelling minstrel gives an account of his wanderings, and a list of kings and tribes he has visited; he tells of the presents he has received, of the honourable reception he has met with, and of the welcome that greeted him on his return. Among the kings whom he mentions as his contemporaries are Hermanric, King of the Visigoths, Attila, and Aelfwine, who is generally believed to be the Alboin who reigned in Italy in the middle of the 6th century. This chronological difficulty is explained away on the one hand by ascribing the names of later date to interpolators, and on the other by assigning the whole poem to the close of the 6th century, or even to a still later period. Again, other critics see indications of great antiquity in the geographical details that Widsith introduces, which seem to point to a time when certain tribes still lived as neighbours on the Baltic shore. A principal element of interest in the poem is the mention of persons who are connected with the chief Teutonic sagas, some of whom, if parts of the poem are as genuinely old as some believe, must have been known to Widsith personally; as Mr. Stopford Brooke writes, "the very possibility that he saw these men (Hermanric and Attila) excites us."   *Ed.*, trans. by Henry Morley, in A. S. Cook and C. B. Tinker's "Select Translations from old English Poetry," 1902: Wülcker, "Kleinere Angelsächsische Dichtungen."   *MS.*, Cod. Ex.

The Lament of Deor, or, *The Minstrel's Consolation*. The only surviving example of an A.-S. poem written in strophic form and with a refrain.

Mr. Stopford Brooke (*op. cit.*) has translated the Lament; the last strophe, which explains Deor's complaint, is given as follows in his version:

"Whilom was I Scôp of the Heodenings:
Dear unto my Lord! *Deor* was my name.

[1] For probable date of early poems, *see* Trautmann (*op. cit.*, under Cynewulf, pp. 121–123).

Well my service was to me many winters through ;
Loving was my Lord ; till at last Heorrenda,—
Skilled in song the man !—seized upon my land-right,
That the guard of earls granted erst to me.
That one overwent ; *this* also may I."

The Heorrenda is thought to be the Horant, known in
"Gudrun," who, according to the description in this of his
powers was "a northern Orpheus" (see interesting note in
"Modern Language Notes," vol. x. No. 2). The poet's
consolation is the thought of the heroes who have suffered and
overcome ; here again are allusions to sagas. Authorities
differ as to whether the composition dates from before the
migration, or from a later period. *Ed.*, trans., A. S. Cook
and C. B. Tinker, *op. cit.* ; Wülcker, *op. cit.* *MS.*, Cod. Ex.

3   The Epic in England.[1]

No work of the epic class is extant dealing with purely
Anglo-Saxon material (Körting). The full development of
the epic in England appears to have been checked by the
introduction of Christianity.

Beowulf, "the oldest heroic poem in a Germanic tongue,"
is founded on Teutonic Myth and Saga.

1st part.   Beowulf's fight with Grendel.
2nd ,,   Beowulf's fight with Grendel's dam.
3rd ,,   Beowulf's return home.
4th ,,   Beowulf's fight with dragon, and death.

A magnificent hall, called Heorot, is built by Hrothgar,
King of the Danes ; here his warriors sleep, but they are
nightly disturbed by a monster, Grendel, who invades the hall
and carries off many of their number. Hearing of Hrothgar's
distress, Beowulf comes to his aid, and after a fierce combat
with Grendel he mortally wounds the monster. The following day there is feasting, and the men retire to rest at night,
believing all danger over, but Grendel's mother, as formidable

---

[1] The Epic is peculiar to the Aryan races. Of the nations whose
literature is dealt with in this volume only the English, the French, and
the Germans, had an early developed epic. *See* G. Paris, "Hist.
poetique de Charlemagne," pp. 2-3.

a foe as her son, comes to avenge his death and seizes one of the chiefs of the Thegns. Beowulf pursues the enemy, even to her dwelling under the water, and there has a terrible encounter with her which ends by Beowulf slaying her with a blow from an elfin sword. Beowulf returns home, and in time becomes king. Fifty years after, he meets his own death in a combat with a dragon, the guardian of an immense treasure, his faithful Wiglaf being the only follower with him at the end.

A mass of controversial criticism has gathered round this poem; space will only allow a reference here to the main arguments.

Beowulf is not known to history, but the Hygelac, of whom Beowulf was the nephew and avenger, has been identified with King Chochilaicus, mentioned by Gregory of Tours, who was killed fighting against the Frisians at some time between 515-520. As this expedition is alluded to in Beowulf, it sets a limit to the date of the origin of the main tale, and as fifty years elapse before the final catastrophe takes place, this brings us to the closing decades of the 6th century, after which a certain time must be allowed for the formation of the original lays on which the later epic was founded. We here approach the point around which controversy has been most lively. Authorities on one side, with Müllenhoff at their head, decided that the poem is a compilation of old lays; Müllenhoff dissected the poem and separated what he considered the different lays from the main text; on the other hand, the Beowulf is believed by Grein and others to be a poem complete in itself, based on older materials, the general opinion being, that the tale had its birth on the Continent, was brought over to us "presumably by the Angles," and assumed its present form on English soil, in the 7th or 8th century. Sarrazin ("Beowulf Studien," pp. 91, 109) gives the poem to Cynewulf, "who based it on an old Danish original." Trautmann opposes him (op. cit., under Cynewulf). The chief actors are Danes and Geats (Goths, of the South of Sweden; identified by some with the Jutes). The scenery described, notwithstanding an attempt made by Haigh ("A.-S. Sagas," 1861) to prove that it is English, is generally conceded to be Scandinavian. Everything is thought to point to the poem having had its birth before the migration of the tribes to this island, and to the Christian elements in the poem being accretions of later growth. According to Bugge we only received back what we gave. "It is evident," he writes, "that the author of Beowulf was familiar with a Christian English poem on the Creation." (*See* "The Home of the Eddic Poems," trans. Schofield, Grimm Library, xi.) The poet who wrought the old materials into the form of the extant version is unknown; Professor Earle traces his name in Hygelac, which he interprets as Higeberht, who was Archbishop of Lichfield under Offa, rejecting the identification with Chochilaicus. Authorities differ as to the locality in which the lays were first welded into a connected poem; some give it a birthplace in Mercia, others in Northumbria. According to Ten Brink the MS. is in the Wessex dialect. The myth of Beowa, the third in genealogical descent from Sceáf, the oldest name in the heathen pedigrees, is blended with that of Beowulf. The idea of a nature-myth underlying the Beowulf legends is accepted by some scholars. There have been different theories as to the origin of the name of Beowulf. Certain placenames in England preserve the memory of the Beowulf saga. "Whatever historians have agreed to recognise as the distinguishing features both of the Teutonic and Scandinavian branches of our race—all these things appear among the incidents of a poem a little over 3000 lines" (Earle).

There are similarities with the "Beowulf" in the Icelandic Grettis Saga (*Ed.*, trans. Magnusson and Morris).

Eds., Heyne, 1863, 67, 73, 79, 7th ed., 1903; Heyne-Socin, 1888, 1898; Zupitza (autotypes of MS.; transliteration and notes), E.E.T.S., 1882; Harrison and Sharp (based on 4th ed., Heyne); Holthausen, 1905; Prose trans., J. M. Kemble, 1833, 35, 37 (two first eds. include "Traveller's Song" and "Battle of Finnes-bush"); T. Arnold, 1876; J. Earle, 1892; J. R. C. Hall, 1901; C. B. Tinker, 1902. Verse trans., Wackerbarth, ballad measure, 1849; Thorpe (with "The Scop, or Gleeman's Tale," and "Fight at Finnesburg") 1855, 1875; Lumsden (modern rhymes), 1881; Garnett, 1885, 4th ed., 1906 (full bibliography); J. L. Hall, 1892, 1900; Morris and

Wyatt, 1895, these in imitative measures; selections in blank verse, Conybeare, "Illustrations of A.-S. Poetry," 1826. For critical notices of above, see C. B. Tinker, "The Translations of Beowulf." For summary of opinions on the various contested points, see Introduction to "Deeds of Beowulf," J. Earle, 1892; and Wülcker, "Grundrisz, etc." (*op. cit.*), 1885. For further information as regards articles in literary journals, and other works, see Trautmann, in Bonner, "Beiträge zur Anglistik," Heft ii. 62, 1899; Körting (*op. cit.*) and Chevalier, *op. cit.*; Th. Krueger, "Geschichte der B. Kritik," 1884. (See Skeat, *Academy*, x. 1876, xxi. 1877, for name of Beowulf.) *MS.*, Cott. Vitell. A. xv., apparently of 10th century, injured by fire.

Battle of Finnsburg. Fragment only. This is part of a saga to which there is a reference in Beowulf. It belongs, like the latter, to the Saga-cycle of the Scandinavian coast region. *Eds.*, Hickes, "Thesaurus." Text with trans., Thorpe, 1855; prose trans. (with "Beowulf"), J. R. Clark Hall, 1901; J. M. Garnett, 1882. Harrison and Sharp (see "Beowulf"); with "Beowulf," by F. Klaeber (Belles Lettres). *MS.*, now lost. Found on a leaf bound up with A.-S. Homilies at Lambeth Library. Known from Hickes's copy.

Waldere. Two fragments — 1st frag., Hildegunde's speech to Walther, encouraging him to fight; 2nd frag., Defiant interchange of speech between Walther and Gunther, preliminary to fight. Hildegunde and Walther are escaping from Attila's court with treasure, when they are attacked by Gunther. These fragments are remains of a song or larger work belonging to the Walther-saga (Burgundian-Hunnish cycle). The A.-S. poem is thought to be founded on a High German original, now lost, probably of first half of 8th century. The fragments agree with an extant version of the Saga, represented by the Latin poem, "Waltharius," the work of Ekkehard i., a monk of St. Gall, who died 973 (*see* Germany, § 8). *Ed.*, "Two leaves of King Waldere's Lay," text and trans., G. Stephens, 1860. *MS.*, 9th century. Found 1860 in Royal Library, Copenhagen.

4 VIITH CENTURY.

668 A.D. Theodore, a Greek of Tarsus, afterwards Archbishop of Canterbury; Hadrian, an African Monk; Biscop Baducing (Benedict Biscop); these three came to England and spread the knowledge of Latin and Greek, and of the Arts and Sciences.

The libraries at the chief seats of learning, in Kent, Wessex, and Northumbria, were enriched by books obtained by pilgrims to Rome.

Schools of York became famous.

Anglian period of English Literature: late 7th to early 9th century. Poetry flourished chiefly in the Anglian districts, but it has not been in all cases transmitted in Northern dialect.

PROSE.

The oldest monuments are compilations of laws. Earliest written laws appeared soon after the coming of St. Augustine.

Kentish Laws. Codes of Aethelberht (d. 616) and his successors, (cir. 601 to cir. 695). Extant in W. Saxon translation.

Laws of Ine (King of W. Saxons, 688–726). The Earliest Laws of Wessex (688-695). Re-issued by King Aelfred. *Ed.*, B. Thorpe, "Ancient Laws and Institutes of England," text and trans., 1840; Liebermann, "Gesetze der Angelsächsen," text and trans. into modern German, 1898, etc., in progress. *MSS.*, Textus Roffensis; Cott. Nero. A. 1, and several others in Cottonian Collection; Harl. 55, and others in Harleian Coll.; C.C.C.C.; Camb. Univ. Libr.; Bodleian; foreign Libraries. For full list of MSS. see Liebermann, *op. cit.*, vol. i. pp. 13–42.

5 Anglo-Saxon Christian poetry begins with—

Caedmon, d. cir. 680. The only information we have concerning this poet is given by Baeda in his "Ecclesiastical History" (Book 4, chap. 24). Caedmon was a lay-brother of the monastery of Streoneshalh (Whitby), under the Abbess